BLUE COUNTRY

A COLLECTION OF SHORT POETRY

NUPUR GOYAL

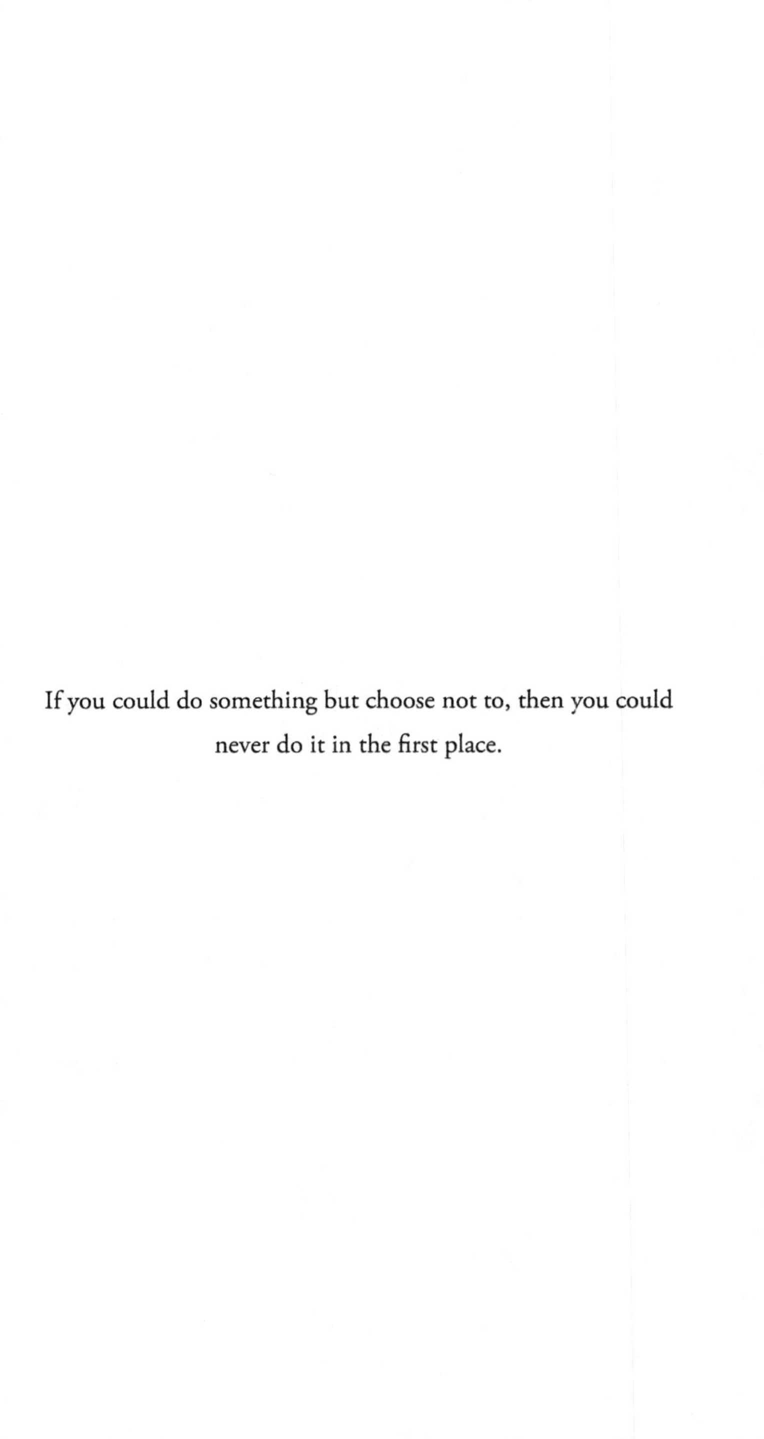

If you could do something but choose not to, then you could never do it in the first place.

Contents

Preface   *vii*

PART I

  1. The Sun   3

  2. 117 Afterparty   4

  3. Spider Lillies   5

  4. Borderline Blue   6

PART II

  5. Handful Of Sand   9

  6. I Just Create Hopes   10

  7. Honey With A Pinch Of Grey   11

  8. Denial   12

  9. Nobody's Home   13

PART III

  10. Backseat   17

  11. A Little Souvenir   18

  12. Unlovable   19

  13. Beyond Imagination   20

PART IV

  14. In A Marble   25

  15. The Pearl   26

  16. Keyframe   27

  17. A Tourist's Haven   29

  18. Warriors   31

Preface

I never thought of writing a book, let alone publishing it. But what I did think of, always, was to write. To write until I could, about whatever I could, in whatever ways I could. So every time I had an influx of emotions that I couldn't explain, I did exactly what I thought I couldn't do- I put them in words. And here I have it, my very own collection of poetry.

When I showed it to my friends, I was fortunate enough to receive their unconditional and unwavering support. Even still, it was extremely hard for me to complete this, given my inherent fear of being judged and criticized. I was afraid that people will not like what I write, one of the only things I really put my heart into, and I would be lying if I say I'm over it now. But I decided to go forward with my first book nevertheless because of all the people who made me feel worthy and confident enough to venture on this journey.

For everyone who has purchased this book, I cannot explain in words how thankful I am for your support. What matters to me the most is that I could share my feelings through my work with others, and this is a feeling that I'll never forget.

PART I

[SUMMER]

1. THE SUN

It who dawns upon the Earth
Zenith of the formless
Thin streaks of golden it casts through the azure canvas
Galvanizing the bleak and enkindling its art
So is the Sun,
Charming yet humble to the life it gives
The source of light and life
The muse of humanity, a labyrinth yet
How miraculous indeed, yet so puzzling
That one could hold so much power
In a minute it could set ablaze yet it chooses
To be the essence of creation
Tranquil like the dawn, idyllic like the dusk
Bliss fills the air when it peeps through the window
Tenderly silhouetted against the blues
Centre of our world, as much as we know
Splashing the canvas with a rosy hue
From the canopy, the twilight shining bright
And like that, it gives way to the night
A harbinger of hopes and new beginnings
Nothing but grateful we are for thee
Cherish with your heart, the serendipity of its existence
For neither is eternal, it or we.

2. 117 AFTERPARTY

A swirling typhoon with a hot core in between
Scattered with thunder that could never be seen
Move along its path and throw your pride aside
Hidden in a blanket is a child sitting inside
Clenching at the daggers and bleeding with one hand
With the other it holds to the ground that withstands
The terror of its agony and pain that was left unchecked
Pacify or regret at the remnants that she wrecked.

3. SPIDER LILLIES

Bloom in autumn so that winters don't feel so cold
Walk on sand so that grass doesn't make you fold
Ring the alarms so that the sun can't burn your hand
Tame the lions so that your horses can fight unmanned
Love so hard that tears can't fill your wounds
Run so fast that the night can't catch up to your dooms
Plough your fields so that rain can't run down your home
Let loose of the strings that abandon you of your freedom
Dusk the ordeals so that you can indemnify the dawn
Pay your tribute to the moments long gone
But don't forget the creek where your shadows dwell
To the long journey they've had, bid them farewell.

4. BORDERLINE BLUE

Once upon a time lived a fish around
So lovely and wonderful, safe and sound
In the golden goldfish bowl that cracked apart
When rays of the sun pierced through the glass
It kept swimming among the broken glass bits
Not ready to part with its 'home' that slit
That shiny skin of hers every time she moved
So she stayed, quiet and unmoved
One day, I picked her up and smiled
Looked her in the eyes and asked, "wanna fly?"
But before it could answer, let alone prepare
I pushed her out in the night sky
And to my surprise, she didn't flinch
As she fell ashore but picked herself right up
And sore through the unchartered with so much zeal
As if this was all what she'd been waiting for
That I thought to myself, why did I ever worry?

PART II

[FALL]

5. HANDFUL OF SAND

With a handful of sand, I wish to walk the dessert
I wonder whether it's my incapacity or its free nature
As it slips through my hand, I am reminded
Of the ones with time, or not really so;
With a handful of sand, my ego is fed
While my feet burn and freeze incessantly
Is it the power that I desperately try to hold onto
Or the vastness of this dessert that is holding onto me;
With a handful of sand, I admire from afar
I run toward the stars, but I am afraid
With my sinking self as I go deeper and deeper
Into the unknown that had me enchanted;
Why must something so barren be so beautiful
Or was it the night sky that had me beguiled
But it's now too late to be off the coast
So, with a handful of sand, this tower I will build.

6. I JUST CREATE HOPES

I just create hopes
Trapped in a life that was doomed to be awry
Building seamless dreams as I glare at the sky
With aims as high as far the eyes could reach
Foreseen future but differently I'd preach
To all my pillars I wish I could tell
How heavy it feels, but I am rather compelled
To just weave what the eyes would admire
So, I just create hopes.

7. HONEY WITH A PINCH OF GREY

It doesn't matter

I'm not the only one groveling

Behind these wild bushes, under the heavy canopies

Every time the slate breaks, I build a new one

Keep it rubbing on the dust until it's ash

And step on the flies that feed on the shrubs

It is a luxury to be seen, and even more to not be

A person in a crowd of imposters is the real criminal

To think I know better, although, is a lie straight up

I can try to be all that everyone knows that I am

But I know that no one is what they and I know that they are

Because everyone has a slate to fill, a plate to break

One steps on another's like it'd fill their plate better

But why would I care, I'm busy groveling

It doesn't matter after all.

8. DENIAL

Today is the day for some hard home truths you say
But where is the home in the truths that hit my face?
When it peels my skin and lays bare my heart
I know I must return to square one, right to the start
I like to protect my sanity, that it what it is
But you say my sanity is not worth the efforts, the time?
Then maybe I should face the hailstorm in place
For all its worth, at least there'll be a speck of reality in my
day.

9. NOBODY'S HOME

To walk into a hollow, empty can, with its heavy air and nothingness
In a black, empty canvas, washed out with every step you take
Outside voices like a distant echo
In a blanket of overwhelming silence
You want to shout but no voice comes out
Words pass over although read thrice out loud
Every day is blank, with no start or end in view
All you wish for someone to sew you right through
How can something so empty be so heavy?
Why wouldn't you stop already?
You gave pieces of you to strangers to take
And now you're left with your neck up a stake
You feel so exhausted, when really you are
Just numb from being ripped apart
And now there's nothing to feel anymore
And that's how, you end up a nobody's home.

PART III

[WINTER]

10. BACKSEAT

The steering wheel feels out of reach
Should I be the one giving directions
Shouldn't I be the one handling the reins?
All of my life I've tried to express
This tornado that I've kept locked inside the doors
Of the shackles that my mind created on its stead
I wonder if I can ever truly be in the body that I claim to own
To not be the audience but to start my own show
To not just be the rock that rolls
On the pavements that other people troll
Is it the intimacy of my incapacity that I fear
Or the rosy bush of taboos that I'm afraid to step in
Either way my feet are covered in mud
To try to wash it off would be in vain
Like the Canterville infamous for its blood stain
But this blood too is not my own
What truly scares me is the final day
When everything I'm made of, everything that's borrowed
Will have to return to its original way
I wonder if there would still be any piece left
That would truly be my own.

11. A LITTLE SOUVENIR

I cannot quite explain the way it tingles me
When I'm left with fragments of your mind
Maybe I've made you too much of my priority
But I just want to throw my worries to the wind behind
When you tell me all about your day
And I sit beside you with my tinkling eyes
To the fact I know it's not this way
Not everyone has the privilege to ride this tide
I love being the shoulder you want to cry on
I love it when there's a you that comes with only us
I love it when I'm the first one you need to call
But my own self haunts me of my bleak shadows
What if the cassette to my demons unrolls
What if you get to know what lies behind these eyes
So very carefully I keep it under folds
I wouldn't want you to strangle, would I?
I know I might not be able to come back to you
Or keep what we have forever as I go
But what if it's all the same this time too
Would you mind if I keep this one as a little souvenir for show?

12. UNLOVABLE

Love is a lie, a disgrace, a disguise
People can love people, just not me
Because loving another takes all of a person
And I am as unlovable as a person could be
I'm as unlovable as the winter moon that hides behind its
spots
As much as the boy sitting on the last seat
I am as unlovable as a dead, wrinkled flower
Devoid of all its fragrance and beauty
I am as unlovable as the piece left undone
By an artist who died a little too early
I am as unlovable as a Monday morning
And the alarm that breaks your sleep
I am as unlovable as a black cat
For a person who's crossing the street
I am as unlovable as that one extra spoon of sugar
For a coffee that's already way too sweet
I can try to be all the things I'm not
Just to please the people around me
But I'll never change, so I'd rather not try
Because I am as unlovable as you could think of me.

13. BEYOND IMAGINATION

I trip upon a book on one strange Sunday night

With it I cover my head and run home

While it had drenches, I felt so much better

My trembling fingers dithering to turn the pages so soaked

They cover felt awfully heavy, but I wasn't the weak

As I read and read and read

To my surprise, which seemed so comfortable to me

I found myself engulfed in its shade

Before I knew, I ran back home every day

Waiting to be intoxicated by its earthly smell of air

That surrounds when I let my doors open

For once I could sit under the night sky

And fall for the falling stars without wishing upon them

But little did I know, this lovely field of daisies

Was not the soil I could till

I tried to protect it, but in fact

I couldn't stand losing it to someone else

After all, wasn't it I who found it first?

But I regret not even a single day

That I spend under the canopy of these forests so gaily

For it made me believe that I too was someone worthy of
being founded by

I wanted to stand on the top of my roof
And scream about my voyage to my heart's content
But instead, I just painted a little something
Because like every other good thing, this too had to end.

PART IV

[SPRING]

14. IN A MARBLE

• 25 •

Is this the life I saw ahead of me?
Is this how I thought my future would be?
If the stars could whisper and the sky could tell
Would they tell me if this will end well?
An autumn noon, the zephyr gently kissing my head
I put it in my everything, my heart that I shred
Intricately woven, I spun my dreams
On the yarn of hope, I'll watch them gleam.

15. THE PEARL

An epitome of amicability, like water in sunlight glistens,
With so heavy a serenity, to the stars, it listens,
Pour your heart out, and sure, it will keep it tight,
Engulfed in its rich inner world, lies a pearl inside.

16. KEYFRAME

Violet hue, the morning dew
The briefest moments when I knew you
Those blossoms of the cherry wood
Wails of my heart that the sky withstood
The aftertaste of wistfulness
The euphony of this mess
You sewed me to a state where I
Could finally seep the esse of sky
That was before me all the time
Just enwrapped by my own grime
But you fabricated all these lies
To intricate feathers in disguise
The warped reality of my dreams
The serenity of the clouds that gleamed
The emotions I thought I had gravened
Hidden inside someone's haven
You alleviated me of my plights
Ecstasy of that momentary delight
I clung onto the hopes you grew
I picturized all the lines you drew
You showed me I could recall
A world beyond these high-built walls
Although it was just a while

I brisked my pace in denial
Delusions of the deep slumber
Oblivious of the thorny blunders
I breathed the flimsy scent you sprayed
I walked the heather path you laid
Then why did you stop singing your song,
When you were inside of me all along?

17. A TOURIST'S HAVEN

To wake up this dawn and see the sun gleam
I pack my bags and leave unsaid
With glitters in my eyes, and clouds in my dreams
Shoes tightened as I prepare for the tread
A little quiet nook in this quiet little corner
Sprinkled with dust but not quite the type to be seen
So enchanting, so appealing to wander
Where affluency flows like morning dew on the green
No rumbles from the stomachs can be far-felt
To each his own, not the way of these folks
Stronger than the bound of a traveller's shoes' welt
Could this be of where the gods bespoke?
Where a man and a woman can both stand tall
And no child is beheld from the wonders of a pen
Where the rills drip of innocence that clean water calls
And available is brightness time and again
Where economy grows gently like a birch tree up a hill
Industry fills the void that the labour creates
Cities are lit up night when the wind flows still
Where one cannot for life spot a niche to berate
Where deers jump with glee and the squirrels squeak
Water is lightened and the fish dance around

When sunrays peep through the canopy of trees
Where life is abundant and everywhere to be found
Such is a place where I want to end
A journey of thousand miles could not suffice
A hope so surreal that could not transcend
The reality check that our world provides
So, I keep on walking and walking without a stop
For somewhere in the world my dreams might surround.

18. WARRIORS

Tis the tale of a land once golden

That took over the sky of hearts and divine

With a heartfelt culture of colours in records

Sowed the seeds of humanity in a field so benign

Until came a hoard of marauders

Ready to strip it of its gold

Tying the people in ropes of order

In the very land they used to call their home

But out they came of their misery

Pulled out their swords and sticks and pens

To write its tryst with destiny

Dragged though the swamp of bloodshed

All the warped history came undone

When we saw the scars these shackles left

Cleansing the fabric in evil so spun

A mountain of challenges ready to address

Now that we had our homeland

On we went on a journey so profound

One by one, picking up the shattered pieces

To rebuild our homes once forgotten or found.

Book cover credits: vansh:)